Ruby's Mountain

Houstine Cooper

RUBY'S MOUNTAIN

Written by Houstine Cooper

Expanded edition @Copyright 2012 Houstine Cooper

All rights reserved. No part of this book may be used or reproduced in any manner whatsoever without prior permission of the author; except in the case of brief quotations embodied in reviews.

Published by
Holton-Dollarhide Publishing
Scotts Valley, California
Holton-Dollarhidepublishing.com
ISBN: 978-0-9893866-0-9

Forward

This book is based on the memoirs of a 93 year old nursing home resident. Ruby Gertrude Holton Bean, my mother, was born in 1895 near Clarksville, Arkansas. Her clear mind and memory of events in her life when she was a child was amazing. She wrote these 'stories' in a book and asked us to read each one every time we visited.

The contrast between the early 1900's and today boggles the mind.

I hope you enjoy the book.

Houstine Cooper

Ruby's Mountain

Chapter 1

Darkness still filled the room when Papa shook her gently this cold winter morning with a whispered,

"Wake up, Ruby girl, time is a-wasting".

She sleepily rubbed her eyes and wished she could lie back down beside her sister in the warm bed. Even at six years old, she knew Papa depended on her to help him with the outdoor chores. Seeing the light from the coal oil lamp in the kitchen, she threw back the covers and stepped onto the cold wooden floor. She turned and made sure Sally was covered and still asleep then glanced toward the smaller bed across the room where Jewell was sleeping soundly. Shivering, she exchanged the pretty flowered flannel night gown for the scratchy woolen underwear. The rest of the day's outerwear was thrown on quickly so she could get to the kitchen warmth. A tangled strand of hair caught on a button on the back of her favorite blue dress. Grabbing her shoes and stockings she hurried to the kitchen for Mama's help. She got her hair loose and ran a quick comb through. She pulled on her long cotton stockings, folding the bottom of the legs of the underwear tightly so the stockings would go over smoothly. She hooked them to the long straps fastened to the waist of the long johns that reached to her upper thigh. Slipping her feet into the high top shoes, she laced them tightly. They felt real good. Mama had her a hearty breakfast of oatmeal, ham and a hot biscuit ready to eat before she went out to the barn to join Papa. Mama helped Ruby on with her long brown wool coat, cap and mittens and she was ready to go. With a quick 'thank you, Mama' Ruby stepped out the back door.

Today they were going to take shelled corn up to the cave on the other side of the woods to feed the hogs wintering there. Papa had the horses saddled and the sacks of shelled corn tied behind. It was still early, but the sun was beginning to peak through the leafless trees. The cold took her breath away. The clean crisp air and the golden glow of the dawn surrounded her.

She stopped.

Ruby's Mountain

Streaks of pink, blue, purple and gold filled the sky. Standing still for a moment she looked around as if seeing the homestead for the first time. It all came into focus: the picnic table, the bucket hanging over the well, the barn with the cow softly lowing inside, the chicken coop with the old red rooster on top, ready to let the world know the sun was growing and day was here. It was as if in another world. "Oh, how she loved this mountain home!"

Exhilarated, she breathed deeply and jumped from the porch. Squealing with happiness she ran across the yard to Papa standing beside the horses.

He smiled and agreed when Ruby cried with delight, "Oh, Papa, what a magical time of a beautiful day!"

Papa lifted her into the saddle. He slung his rifle strap across his shoulder, mounted his horse and they started out of the barnyard.

Her horse trotted closely behind Papa's on the narrow familiar deer trail. Sunlight flooded the sky now and the woods seemed to come alive. A noisy crow flew overhead and squirrels chattered as they jumped from tree to leafless tree. The wonder of it all filled her heart with happiness as nothing else could. "I never want to leave this mountain" she thought, "never in a million years could I be so happy anywhere else." She realized that in spite of the warm woolen mittens her mother had knitted for her, that her hands were cold. She was about to call to papa when he stopped his horse.

"Shhh"

Holding his finger to his lips Papa quietly took the rifle from his shoulder and aimed. She jumped at the crack of the shot and saw the fawn he had so quickly felled. He dismounted, gathered the small deer and put it across Ruby's horse in front of her saddle as the doe disappeared into the woods.

"Mama will be so pleased to have some fresh meat to cook," she muttered as she ran her cold hands through the soft warm fur. In her mind she went to the root cellar to get potatoes, carrots and rutabagas to cook with the delicious roast. "Maybe Mama will make fried apple pies, too!" There were still some dried apples she had helped peel and slice last fall. Again that wonderful feeling of thankfulness and belonging came over her. Soon they reached the creek and fence separating them from the hogs pinned in the cave.

Papa lifted her from the saddle before he started feeding. She jumped up and down swinging her arms to get warm. They laughed as the squealing, grunting, hungry hogs pushed each other from the trough.

"We brought enough for all," remarked Ruby as if talking to the greedy hogs. After a short stay,

Papa lifted her into the saddle and they started back the way they came toward home. They stopped for Papa to dismount and inspect the few cattle left in the woods on their return. "They are doing fine", he declared as he got back on his horse.

He had taken a boxcar load of cows and one of hogs to Kansas City to sell early in the fall. Several men had helped him round them up and drive them to the Clarksville depot. He rode in the caboose so he would be there when they unloaded at the stockyards. It took about a week for him to complete his business. While he was gone Ruby fed the chickens, gathered the eggs and helped feed the other animals while Mama milked the cow left behind in the barn. One day Mama made chicken and dumplings, hot biscuits and opened a jar of green beans that were canned in early spring. What a delicious change from the root cellar vegetables they had eaten since Papa had been gone.

Jewell helped carry in wood for the cook stove and fireplace. Mama drew most of the water from the well and Ruby carried it into the house. Some times she wondered if the big wooden bucket by the door and the hot water reservoir on the side of the cook stove would ever get full, especially when it was raining.

When her horse stopped abruptly, Ruby realized they were home. She helped feed and water the horses then headed for the back door.

Ruby's Mountain

"Mama, we got you some fresh meat," Ruby said as she burst in through the back door.

"I am so glad, Ruby," she replied. "Now get over by the stove, take off your coat and mittens and get warm."

Ruby was very thankful for the warm kitchen and a loving mother.

Chapter 2

"Papa! Papa! The bees are here! The bees are here!"

Ruby shouted, her voice ringing with excitement as she raced toward the barn.

The bright warm sun and slight cool breeze said quietly, 'spring is here'. The children were out playing with only a sweater to keep them warm. The pan of sugar sweetened corn cobs Papa had set on the table in the back yard was covered with honey bees.

Ruby's Mountain

Papa was sharpening a plow but stopped pedaling the grindstone to meet Ruby at the barnyard gate.

"The bees have come, Papa", she repeated.

"Get me some flour."

Ruby ran to the back porch where Mama, hearing the excitement, had a cup of flour waiting for her.

"Stand back all of you," Papa said as he crept slowly to the table. He reached out with a hand full of flour and with as little motion as possible sprinkled it on the back of the bees. They lifted in the air as if they were all one and flew off toward the woods with Papa close behind. The flour made them more visible among the trees that were just beginning to leaf out.

"I want to go," Ruby whined watching him disappear into the woods.

"No," replied Mama, who had joined the group to keep them away from the table.

"You can go with him tomorrow". Ruby turned away reluctantly.

Papa returned in about an hour and enthusiastically announced he had found the bee tree and marked the way to return tomorrow.

Ruby's Mountain

Ruby shivered as the warm sun went behind a cloud and the cool spring breeze ruffled her hair. She shifted from one foot to the other while impatiently waiting for Papa to finish plowing the shallow trenches. Old Bart, pulling the plow, seemed to be moving even slower than usual.

"I want to go now," she had told Papa early this morning.

"We will go collect the honey after we finish planting those peas," he assured her.

Jewell jumped up and down and kicked dirt clods beside Ruby, not really wanting to work.

"Finally," she muttered as they picked up the syrup buckets with the swollen peas and started down the row. Mama had soaked the seed last night so they would sprout quicker and they must not dry out before they are covered in the rows.

They had only covered a few feet when the kitchen door slammed and out ran Sally, yelling as she ran on her pudgy little legs.

"Me help, me help,"

Jewell set her bucket down roughly, spilling some peas, and ran to Sally. They grabbed hands and started jumping around singing 'ring around the Rosie'.

"Jewell, stop that now and get back to your job," Ruby screamed with frustration.

Ruby's Mountain

Papa came out of the house to see what the ruckus was all about.

"Papa, I just want to hurry and get through so we can go get the honey," Ruby explained with a whine in her voice.

"Sally, go back inside and Jewell pick up your bucket and get busy".

"Yes, Papa."

"And as for you, Ruby, the harsh screaming is not necessary. We will go soon as you are finished and not before."

"Yes, Papa," she said and started walking faster down the middle between the rows of trenches.

Papa already had the clean buckets and torch fixed when she was ready. The long handled torch was made of old rags wound tightly around a green tree branch. It was for Ruby to hold, lighted, to keep the bees off Papa while he collected the honeycomb filled with honey from the tree he will cut down.

They ate a small dinner and took off for the woods.

Ruby giggled as Papa spread his arms pretending to be a monster.

"Oh, Papa, you are so funny!"

Ruby's Mountain

They had stopped a short distance from the bee tree to put on the protective garb: flowing net over their hats to cover past the shoulders, heavy gloves and long sleeve over-shirts.

"You look pretty funny yourself!" Papa teased.

The extra garb was to protect them from being stung when Papa cut down the tree and scraped the honeycomb into the buckets.

By middle of the afternoon they were on their way home when Papa stopped and set his buckets down. Ruby did, too, and wondered why he had stopped, but welcomed the break.

"See that patch of plants over there", he asked her.

"Where, Papa?"

"They aren't very tall, but you can tell they are all the same kind close together and a different shade of green than the ones around them."

"Now I see them."

"We will mark this spot and come back later to gather the May apples to eat and the poison roots to dry and take down to the general store for Mr. John to pulverize and sell. But now, we better get home so Mama won't be worried about us".

Ruby's Mountain

He took a small chip out of the tree bark with his hatchet and another one just below. Picking up the full syrup buckets of honey they started on their way. Ruby was glad Mama had wrapped an old piece of towel around the bucket handles to make them easier to hold when full. They were heavy even though they were not filled to the brim.

"Mama, Mama, look how much honey we got!" Ruby said, showing the pails to her, "and not a single sting"!

"That is wonderful. Won't that taste good on a hot biscuit with some fresh butter?" replied Mama.

Ruby set the buckets on the table and sat down.

"We found some May apples, and will go back later to get them, Papa said," she told Mama.

"That will be nice," Mama replied, "now could you please go check on Jewell and Sally, then tomorrow we can seal the honey in jars to put in the root cellar."

"Yes, Mama," she replied, as she went out the back door to find her sisters. She found them at the picnic table in the yard playing counting games with rocks and was glad to join them for a few minutes rest.

Chapter 3

"June, and it is already hot as a firecracker." Ruby heard Papa say as he mopped his brow with a rough cotton handkerchief. He came out of the garden and sat down at the picnic table in the shade of the big oak tree near where the girls had their playhouse.

"Can't I help you with the hoeing, Papa?"

"No, thank you anyway, Ruby," he answered. "It is about time to go after those May apples and look for some ginseng, though."

Ruby's gray eyes got big and bright with anticipation.

Ruby's Mountain

"When, Papa, when can we go?"

"We'll go tomorrow after we pick the turnip greens and the few peas that are ready."

Ruby made a face showing her disappointment but said nothing as he continued.

"The potatoes are getting pretty heavy with bugs, too, but you and Jewell can pick them off late this evening. I'll get the cans of coal oil for you to put them in."

"Yuck!"

This was the very worst job Papa had her do.

When the supper dishes were cleared, Ruby and Papa sat down at the table to work on her reading and arithmetic.

"I borrowed some more books from the teacher at Strawberry," Papa said casually as he handed her a small stack of books from the chair next to him.

"And you didn't tell me?" her voice rising.

"I wanted you to read them for me first," with a twinkle in his eyes.

Picking up one of the books she started to read. Stumbling on a word, she pointed to it and showed Papa across the table. Without hesitation he told her, though the book was upside down to him.

"Papa, I want to read as good as you some day."

"You will be even better, just keep reading every day and learning new words," he replied.

After a few more pages of reading, Papa told her to put the book down and do her arithmetic. She had a new tablet and pencil and worked the problems he gave her with enthusiasm.

"Time for bed," Papa said as he stood preparing to blow out the coal oil lamp. Ruby gathered the books, pencil and tablet then put them in the book satchel Mama had made.

"Thank you, Papa, for helping me and I will help you tomorrow," as she made her way to the bedroom. Sally was already asleep when she crawled in beside her. Ruby felt like she would explode with happiness as the luckiest girl in the world to have such a wonderful family. She drifted off to sleep smiling.

Ruby was up with the sun, eager to get the garden chores done. Papa had the horses saddled and ready to go when she carried the last pan of greens into the house.

"Thank you, Ruby and be careful," Mama said as Auntie came into the kitchen. She was glad

Auntie had come to help while Mama wasn't feeling well.

"You're welcome, Mama," as she ran from the house, slamming the door behind her.

"We will check on the cows and hogs while we are out. With all the acorns, nuts and new vegetation they should be about ready to take to market," Papa said as he boosted her into the saddle. She had the empty flour sacks and he had his rifle and a shovel.

They didn't talk much and the rhythmic jog of the horse as she followed Papa was comforting. Memories and dreams flooded her head.

"I'm almost nine now and love my family and home on this mountain. When we go down to the church at Fort Gibson, or just to Mr. John's store, though, I want more. I hardly know how to talk to others my age and want to learn their games. When Auntie was here before we got baby Edna. Does her visit now mean we are getting another baby?"

Papa stopped his horse to count the small herd of cattle ahead. She watched as Papa dismounted and walked among the cows.

"They are in good shape and the strays as well. The hogs are fat and in their prime, he announced. "Now let's go find what we came for!"

This got her attention and she clicked to her horse and pulling the reins to get him started, turned to follow Papa. In her daydreaming she had not noticed how deep into the woods they had come.

"Damp and cool and not much sunlight," Papa called to her. "Keep your eye out for the May apples; this is where they grow best."

"Over there, Papa, I see some!"

Papa held the horse while Ruby slid from the saddle with the flour sacks and ran to catch up with him.

His shovel sank deep into the decayed leaves around the plants being careful to leave part of the roots. He was very selective and dug only the plants that were drooping with age.

"There aren't as many as I had hoped for, and the few ginseng plants I see are not near ready," he said. "We had better wait a while longer to make sure they are mature."

He put the few May apple plants in one of the flour sacks, boosted her into the saddle and they started back home, quiet in their disappointment.

Papa took the few plants, washed the dirt off and spread them on top of the chicken coop to dry out of reach of the children.

Ruby went in the kitchen to tell Mama and Auntie and help with preparing supper. She was in a hurry to get back to her lessons.

"Do we go get ginseng today, Papa?" Ruby had been marking each day on the calendar hanging on the kitchen wall for two weeks.

"Yes, it should be ready by now", as he rose from the breakfast table. "Draw water for Auntie and finish your chores. We can leave when you get ready."

Ruby was impatient and told the little ones to hurry and finish eating as she gathered the dirty dishes. The water in the tea kettle was boiling, so she ran to the well for water to add. The well water cooled the dish water down so she could swish the lye soap before adding the dishes.

"I can do these dishes", Auntie came up behind her. "You get your flour sack and go with your Papa. He is waiting for you."

"Thank you, Auntie. You are so good to us."

She made two more trips to the well to make sure the kettle on the stove and the wooden tub with the dipper on the wash stand by the door were full. Then with a loud 'thank you' to Auntie she grabbed the flour sack and ran out the back door to join Papa. She stepped into Papa's laced

Ruby's Mountain

fingers and he boosted her into the saddle. They took off for the woods where they had seen the ginseng plants earlier.

Following behind Papa on the trail, she still felt the same contentment as years before and so very happy to be part of this family and this beautiful mountain called Pilot Rock.

At the first group of plants, she slid off the horse with the flour sack. Papa was already inspecting them and deciding which ones to take and which ones to leave for next year. She held the sack open wide for him to put in the whole plant. They would wash the plants thoroughly when they got home and spread them on the table in the back yard to dry. Papa had not let her touch the poison May apple plants, but she wanted to help with the ginseng.

"Papa, when you take these roots to Mr. John's, can I go with you?" she asked as he added another plant to the sack.

"Yes, I will have to take the wagon. Your Mama has a long list of supplies we need and you can help. I hope Mr. John has the bundle of wool she ordered in the early spring. You girls are outgrowing your coats and mittens faster every year."

Ruby giggled and said,"thank you, Papa. She is teaching me to spin, but it is too hot to stay inside now!"

Ruby's Mountain

There were numerous ginseng plants in each place they stopped so the flour sacks were filled quickly.

The next two weeks Ruby watched the ginseng closely, turning the plants every day as the hot sun drew the moisture from the roots. She covered them with an old oil cloth table cloth when a brief summer shower came suddenly one day.

"They will be all right, Ruby," called Mama from the back door as she kept straightening the cloth and getting soaked in the process.

"But I want them to hurry and dry", she called back to her mother.

The two weeks waiting for the ginseng to dry seemed an eternity. She was very anxious to go to Mr. John's store with Papa. Ruby watched Mama's list grow every day and worked harder to care for Sally and Edna and help Papa with the chores. Between chores Mama set aside the spinning of the wool to teach Ruby to sew dresses for herself and her sisters, using the colorful flour sacks she had saved.

"Tuck the bed spread under the mattress, Ruby, then go to the other side of the bed and pull it as tight as you can so there are no wrinkles and tuck it under the mattress also. This will make a firmer surface to lay the material and knives on for cutting." Mama instructed, but did not stoop over to help.

"Yes, Mama".

Mama showed her how to lay the sacks so the pretty flower patterns all went in the same direction. Then she laid the pattern pieces made of newspaper on the sacks and put the case knives on them to hold them in place while she cut.

Ruby picked up the scissors and started whacking away, not very carefully.

"Slow down, Ruby, these pieces you are cutting out have to fit together", she directed from her chair.

"Yes, Mama."

The bright summer day was beautiful and Ruby wanted to be outside playing with Jewell, Edna and Sally.

Mama took the scissors and straightened the cut edges and showed Ruby where to pin them together so Mama could stitch them on the treadle sewing machine. She watched as the pieces came together and started looking like a dress. Mama held it to Ruby every now and then to see if it would fit. Finally as the last pieces of the material were stitched together, she marked where the buttons needed to go at the back neck opening. Mama had noticed how Ruby was paying more attention to the girls outside than watching her put the dress together.

"Go outside and play with your sisters," Mama told her with a smile, "You can sew the buttons on tomorrow".

"Thank you, Mama, I will".

Chapter 4

"Aren't you going with us to church today, Mama?" Ruby asked.

Auntie had made breakfast and Mama was sitting by the table with a light robe over her nightgown.

"Not today, honey, I don't feel well. Papa will take you girls and you will eat dinner with the Terry's after church as usual."

"But, Mama."

Ruby's Mountain

"No buts about it, Ruby. Mind your manners and take care of your sisters. Edna may get cranky after dinner, so lay down with her on a pallet like you do at home and get her to sleep. Now run along and see if your sisters are ready to go. Papa has the wagon hitched and out front. Your new dress we made last week looks real nice."

The compliment helped Ruby feel a little better.

"Thank you." She said and smiled at Mama. She was pleased thinking of how this was the first full dress she had made with Mama's help. It had taken several of the pretty flour sacks Mama had saved.

"I am growing so tall" she mused, "but I have learned fast this summer. Best of all Mama let me sew all the seams on the brand new Singer treadle sewing machine. What fun! Now when it gets cooler I can learn to spin the wool and weave a blanket." But it just was not like Mama to miss church.

Ruby concentrated on getting her sisters ready for church. After they were dressed she took two quilts out and spread them carefully in the bed of the wagon so the younger girls wouldn't have to sit on the splintering wood.

Sitting next to Papa on the spring seat was another real treat and sign she was growing up. But she couldn't help noticing how preoccupied and quiet he was. He seemed to be in a big hurry and kept urging the team to go faster, even to trot on the level places going down the hill. Such a beautiful day and still feeling good about her new dress and bonnet, she was willing to take more time and enjoy the ride and beauty all around.

"We aren't late, Papa." Ruby became more and more puzzled when he didn't answer.

Soon as Papa stopped the wagon at the church he told Ruby to get Jewell, Sally and Edna out of the back while he talked to Mrs. Terry. Ruby tried to hear what he was saying, but was too far away. His urgency and serious face had her so confused. "I sure wish I knew what was happening," she thought. The Terry girls came running and interrupted her speculation.

"We get to play all day," they were so excited they sounded like a chorus, with both girls speaking at the same time.

"You all go home with Mrs. Terry after church and I will pick you up later," Papa said as he climbed back into the wagon. "Be good and take care of your sisters, Ruby," he called. The team took off again in a trot.

"Come along, girls," Mrs. Terry called as they heard the gathering bell ring.

Ruby's mind wandered and at times she could not focus on the sermon. When they all sang 'Shall We Gather at the River' and 'Sweet By and By'

Ruby's Mountain

she joined in and felt comforted despite the confusion she was feeling.

With Mr. and Mrs. Terry up front and all the girls in the back of the wagon, Maydie told Ruby about gathering mulberries and baking the pie they were having for dinner. Both girls laughed when Maydie told her about how black the crust was – "and not burned!"

When all were seated and the blessing said by Mr. Terry, Nora announced she did not want pie, she wanted cake. Mrs. Terry explained that there was no cake, just mulberry pie today. Everyone around the table became very quiet as Nora kept raising her voice and demanding cake.

Ruby gulped in disbelief and shook her head at Jewell and Sally as Nora jumped up from the table, knocked over her water glass and stormed out the back door, slamming it hard.

"I will find her later, finish your dinner," Mrs. Terry said quietly as she mopped up the water with a dish towel.

Edna climbed down from her chair stacked with books and went to sit in Ruby's lap. She was asleep even before everyone had finished eating. Ruby laid her on the pallet Maydie had made for her and went to dry the dishes for Mrs. Terry.

"Where did Papa rush off to?"

"He said he had some things to take care of, dear," was all Mrs. Terry would say.

Nora had not reappeared by the time the dishes were done and put away so Ruby and Maydie went searching for her. They found her sprawled out on the woodpile.

"You can come in now," as they tried to lift her.

"Don't bother, I'm already dead," Nora replied.

Everyone laughed at her dramatics. But when Ruby and Maydie started back into the house she came running, glad to come inside and play with the other children.

Toward sunset Papa came after the girls and was unusually quiet again on the way home. All of Ruby's confusion which had been eased while she was helping Mrs. Terry and playing with the other children came rushing back.

As Papa stopped in back of the house, Auntie appeared in the kitchen door holding a bundle in her arms.

"Come meet your new baby brother," she called to them. Her sisters jumped from the wagon and ran to see while Ruby collected the quilts to bring inside. She was stunned but understood now why Papa had been so serious.

"Where is Mama?" she asked, pushing past Auntie.

"She is asleep, don't wake her," Auntie said sternly. "You can see her tomorrow."

"How could she not tell me? She looks so beautiful with her golden hair spread on the pillow," Ruby cried. With tears in her eyes, angry and hurt she stood in the doorway. "I'm old enough to have Mama's confidence. Auntie is so good to explain things and read stories about what I ask, she could have told me, too."

Ruby turned and ran through the house and out into the back yard when she could no longer control the tears.

"Why didn't she tell me she was going to have another baby? Why? Why? Why?", she anguished as tears rolled down her cheeks. She sat alone on the bench at the table a long time. The ache and confusion would not go away.

Papa finally came and sat down beside her. Her sobbing gradually stopped and she turned to him. He took her hand and speaking softly, told her not to be angry with her mother. "She knows how much you do for all of us and did not want to burden you with the thought of having another baby to help care for."

"Thank you, Papa. I could never stay angry at Mama. I will help as much as I can," she sniffled. "I know a new baby needs a lot of attention."

Papa continued in a soft voice, "Auntie is staying a while longer and will do most of the work. Ruby, girl, I am depending on you. This old farm up here on the mountain we love needs both of us to keep it going. Jewell, Sally and Edna need you to help them adjust to the new baby. His name will be Carl and you will love him as much as you do Edna."

The sun went down and as dusk gathered round them, they sat quietly, holding hands, each in their own thoughts. The tree frogs and the locusts sang their nightly chorus. The evening star was visible and peace settled over their mountain home. Jewell opened the back door and called them to supper. Papa drew water so Ruby could wash her face at the well before they went inside.

After supper Auntie took Papa's place at helping Ruby and Jewell with reading, spelling and arithmetic while Papa went to the bedroom to sit with Mama. Sally and Edna climbed into their chairs and Ruby gave them a pencil and paper to do their 'lessons'.

Ruby couldn't keep her mind on the lessons and was making too many mistakes in her spelling and arithmetic. Auntie closed the books and bade all the girls 'goodnight'. Jewell, Sally and Edna gave her a hug and with a quick 'goodnight' went to their bedroom. Ruby clung to Auntie for several minutes before she said 'nite' and went to the small bedroom where the girls were already in bed. She joined them and understood why Edna's bed had been moved from Mama and Papa's room. Now baby Carl had to have the cradle.

A hint of light from the kerosene lamp in the kitchen was coming through the open door. Ruby undressed, put on her nightgown and lay down beside Sally, being careful not to wake her. There in the darkness her thoughts went over the events of the day. Papa's quiet urging of the team, Nora's outburst and her own reaction to the baby when they arrived home. She was hurt that they had not confided in her, but she decided, she really was the luckiest girl in the world. She had a family that loved and depended on her. Their beautiful mountain was the best place in the whole wide world to live. A shiver ran through her when she thought of the healthy baby brother now added to the family. Smiling there in the darkness she drifted happily into sleep.

Chapter 5

"Whoa"

Papa pulled on the reins to stop by the back yard nearest the kitchen door. He and Ruby had been to Mr. John's store to take the dried ginseng roots and buy supplies. The sunshine and light breeze made the trip down the mountain very enjoyable. On the way home he had let the team travel at their own slow speed so he and Ruby could talk. They sang hymns and laughed at the fussing of squirrels being chased by birds from limb to limb. Papa teased Ruby about calling Pilot Rock her own mountain.

"But you love it up here where the air is clean and the sun seems brighter as much as I do," she replied.

"That I do, girl, that I do."

He set the brakes and stepped out onto the wheel before jumping to the ground. After lifting Ruby down they started unloading the wagon. Papa carried the heavy sugar and flour. While Ruby carried in the material and bundle of wool Mama had ordered, Papa took the team to the barn.

"That was a really good ginseng harvest this year," Mama said as Ruby walked in the door.

"Yes, it was, Mama, and Papa got a good price for it at Mr. John's, so we got everything on your list. Mrs. Johns was in the store and helped me pick out some pretty calico for all us girls a dress and the flowered flannel for night gowns. She also said to tell you 'hello' and hoped to see you and baby Carl soon."

"Thank you, Ruby. Will you please put the supplies away? Auntie and I have our hands full with these apples you and Papa picked yesterday."

Just then angry screams were heard from the back yard.

Mama sighed, "First will you go find out what Jewell and Sally are fighting about now? They have been at odds all day and I don't want to go out there again. See if you can settle them down."

"OK, Mama".

Ruby put the bundles she was carrying on the floor against the wall so they wouldn't be in the way. When she sat down at the picnic table in the back yard Edna climbed up next to her and leaned her head on Ruby's arm.

"Now," Ruby said, "Jewell you and Sally run around the house one time then come sit across from us at the table." The log house was large and by the time they had run all around and back to her they were giggling and whispering like they were good friends again.

"Ruby, do you think we should tell Auntie that the geese are on the other side of the house?"

For some reason the geese did not like Auntie and always pinched the back of her legs before she could get up the steps and into the house.

"You can tell her, but also tell her I will get the water for her in a little while." Ruby said, knowing it takes a lot of water when canning.

Jewell went to the back door and delivered the message.

"Thank you, Jewell."

Auntie started down the back steps just as the geese came around the corner. All the girls saw them at the same time and jumped running and yelling at them to go away. All except the big old white gander scattered and he just kept coming with his wings laid back and his neck stretched with his big orange beak open. Ruby picked up a small stone and threw at him. That slowed him down for a minute, but he came at Auntie again. "Get back on the porch, Auntie," yelled Ruby, "I will get the water!" Jewell picked up a stick at the edge of the yard and came running to hit the gander. He saw her and decided it was time to leave, for this time. All gave a big sigh of relief. Ruby drew the water and carried it in for Auntie, then sat back down with the girls.

"Why can't you, Jewell and Sally, get along and work together like you just did all the time?" Ruby asked. They looked at each other and laughed then to Ruby, "we don't know what you are talking about". She asked them to stop their arguing and upsetting Mama. "Promise," she told them "and come to me if you can't agree again. Then she reached in her pocket and gave each of them and Edna a small piece of candy she had brought back from Mr. John's.

Ruby went back into the house and started storing the supplies she and Papa had brought from the store. Next time Mama or Auntie needed water, she went after it for them.

Hard to believe Carl is a year old already. Ruby was sitting at the table in the back yard peeling potatoes for Mama to cook for supper and watching Carl. The three girls were playing in the other side of the yard and laughing as they 'visited' each other in their pretend separate homes. They each had outlined their 'house' with rocks and used sticks about two feet long to mark their front door. When someone came calling these sticks had to be swung away as a real door before the visitor could enter. Each girl had their rag dolls and pocket dolls as their children. With beds, tables and chairs all marked clearly, they were in a fantasy world all their own.

Carl toddled toward the woods that were so pretty right now.

"Come back, Carl" Ruby called. He looked around at her, laughed and tried to run away. She dropped her knife in the pan of potatoes. Running she scooped him up in her arms just as Papa drove into the yard.

"Look who is here Carl, Papa is home from the store".

"Hi, Papa".

He jumped down from the wagon and took the jumping Carl from her arms.

"Pa, Pa, Pa, Pa", as he snuggled to Papa's chest.

Chapter 6

The light from the crackling fire in the fireplace lit the whole room. The shadows gaily danced and played on the walls and ceiling as the silently falling snow continued to swirl outside.

Ruby, Jewell and Sally sat with legs folded on the pallet. They watched Papa closely as he sat in his chair close by and shook the popcorn popper over the open fire to keep the corn from burning.

Papa had made the popper last year from new screen wire and a heavier single wire around the top. Another piece of the heavy wire around the flat lid of screen wire extended into the long wooden handle. The latches at the edge of the lid caught into the wire around the top of the bowl, holding them firmly together through the vigorous shaking over the fire. The girls squealed with delight when the kernels began bursting furiously.

Edna and Carl, covered with the colorful quilt Mama had finished last week, slept peacefully on the pallet behind the three girls.

"Papa, that red corn from the back of our garden sure pops good." Ruby remarked.

"Yes, it does, Ruby, and there are not many old maids left in the bowl. Now, go get the wooden bowl and salt, this batch is done and we can eat it while I pop some more for the popcorn balls."

Mama left her loom by the window and moved closer to join them.

Ruby scurried to the kitchen. She moved a chair close and stood on it to reach the top shelf in the cabinet for the bowl used only for popcorn.

"We're having a party", she sang as she whirled around the room with the bowl before sitting down again.

It was always fun time when they could all be together in the middle of the day. Her antics woke Edna and Carl who expected to be fed also. Mama picked up baby Carl and held him close so she could nurse him. Edna joined the other girls before the fire to play with her doll.

Ruby started singing Away in a Manger. They all joined in even though Christmas was past. They all knew the song, so no one objected. Then Jewell suggested a song, then Sally and so around the room. By then all the first batch of popcorn had been eaten and Papa declared the next one was done.

Mama laid Carl back on the pallet and went to the kitchen to stir up the makings for the candy to make the popcorn balls. She lit the coal oil lamp and added a stick of wood to the fire in the cook stove. Into the large clean stew pot on the stove she carefully measured one cup sugar, one cup molasses, one fourth cup of water and one teaspoon vinegar. After she stirred and started it cooking she called Ruby to help with the constant stirring necessary. Mama put the large cookie sheet on the table and greased it with lard. Next she measured a tablespoon of butter from the bowl on the table to be ready to add to the mixture on the stove in about twenty minutes. After fifteen minutes of cooking she started testing, by dropping a small amount from the tip of the spoon into a cup of cold water. If it held together in a soft ball when taken from the water with her fingers, it was ready for the butter. She tested every two or three minutes so each of the girls got to eat one of the testers. Mama called Papa in to lift the heavy hot stew pot and pour the mixture over the popped corn in the big bowl while she quickly stirred it with a wooden spoon to coat each kernel. After a few minutes of cooling, the fun for all of them began.

"Rub plenty of butter on the palm of your hands," Ruby instructed. "Now get a handful of the corn and make it into a ball". She laid her ball on the prepared cookie sheet.

Jewell and Sally formed the balls into different shapes as quickly as they could and laughed as they showed everyone their creations. Edna made smaller balls with her little hands and laughed as she tried to make a dog.

After the cleanup they all ate one ball before Papa had to go out into the storm to do chores.

No matter how bad the weather, the horses, hogs and chickens had to be fed. The cows ate as Papa milked. He gathered the eggs from the nests and broke the ice on the watering trough so they could all get a drink.

"Can I help you, Papa?" asked Ruby.

"No, you just stay inside out of this weather. I need you well when this storm is over so we can get some more studying done." Papa explained, and winked at Mama. Ruby was puzzled by the wink, but did not ask questions.

A few days later the storm had passed and the sun came out bright and clear though still cold. The snow had left most of the back yard a large mud puddle. The children were not allowed to get out and play.

"Ruby, the ash bucket is completely full and the ashes need to be taken out of the fireplace again," Mama said. "Would you please take the bucket out to the hopper?"

Ruby laid down her book with a slow "yes, Mama."

Jewell ran to the back door and held it open for Ruby struggling with the heavy bucket of ashes.

"Thank you, Jewell"

The bright sunshine and cold crisp air was very invigorating. Breathing deep she muttered, "Late winter and early spring is such a wonderful time of wondering and planning".

Carefully she stepped off the last step onto the board Papa had laid over the mud puddle. After taking the few steps on the board to the ash hopper she sat the bucket down. It took both hands to lift the lid and set it aside. The odor of stale ashes that had been collected all winter was very strong.

"Yuck", she gagged, and started pouring her new ashes on top. The dust that rose as she quickly added the new bucket full made her cough. She lifted the heavy lid back over the top and made sure it was tight.

Turning to go back into the house she lost her balance and fell back against the hopper and one foot went into the mud before she could catch herself. Mama was watching from the kitchen window and ran to the back door.

"Are you all right, Ruby" she called anxiously.

"Yes, Mama, but I stepped in the mud", Ruby replied disgustedly.

"Bring the bucket and come in, I will help you clean your shoes."

"Sure will be glad when this mud dries up so we can start watering these ashes down and catching the drippings." She remarked aloud to herself. "Mama has enough hog lard already to add to them to make a batch of lye soap. We have used a lot more soap this winter, seems like. I get to stir it in the big kettle after Papa gets the fire going and I like that." She smiled as she carefully walked on the boards back to the porch.

Ruby stopped on the porch and looked at the leafless trees silhouetted against the clear blue sky and all the mud shining in the bright sunshine before removing her shoes. The feeling of awe and happiness swept over her again as it had so many times in the past few years they had lived here. She took another deep breath of the clean cold air before going inside to continue reading her book, with glimpses of worlds away from her beloved mountain.

Chapter 7

    Carl wore a dark blue sweater Mama had knitted for him over the summer as he ran here and there picking up and throwing rocks. The bright golds and reds of the maple trees and deep red of the sumac bushes beside the green pines and cedars visible from the back yard table filled Ruby with overwhelming peace. Tangled vines amid the brown corn stalks in the garden are still showing a green leaf. They are still holding the field peas almost ready to be harvested. The rest of the garden had long ago made many delicious satisfying meals for the family last summer. The remainder had been canned at the peak of freshness for the family's use during the long winter months ahead.

Ruby sat at the table like she had so many times before, watching Carl play. At two he seemed to be growing before her eyes. The bright warm sunshine and light cool autumn breeze set her to dreaming and wondering. What would it be like to start to school? In the book she had just read, the children her age were all being fitted with new clothes and excited about returning to school after summer vacation.

"No, Carl, no", she yelled as she quickly got up and ran after him. At two years old, he was into exploring everywhere he could get away with. Climbing the fence looked like a good idea.

"You little booger, you know you can't go into the chicken coop".

He giggled but was not angry or combative when she scooped him up and held him close on the way back to the table.

"You just wanted me to notice you, didn't you?"

He laughed out loud and grabbed her around the neck.

She stood him beside her on the bench and showed him how to stack the blocks Papa had made. He batted them down and laughed as Ruby tried to catch them before they scooted off the table.

"Now you stack them", she instructed. Instead, he picked one up and threw it at her, just missing her ear as she ducked.

"Why, you little stinker, I'll get you", as he scrambled down off the bench and started to run. He was laughing so hard he stumped his toe and fell.

Just then Mama called from the back door to bring him in for his nap.

"And this dress is ready for you to whip the hem in so bring your book", she added.

Ruby picked up Carl with one big swoop and nuzzled his neck to make him laugh some more on the way to the back door.

Ruby removed his sweater, took Carl to the potty and gave him a glass of milk before laying him in the cradle. He fussed and called after her when she went into the front room, so she took a chair from the kitchen and set it at the foot of the cradle so he could see her.

"Thank you, Mama, for making my dress," she said as she went to be close to Carl with needle, thread and her dress in hand. It was only a few minutes before he settled down and his heavy eyelids closed. The fresh air and exercise had used all his energy.

She covered him with a crib quilt and quietly took her sewing to the kitchen where Mama was getting ready to fix supper. She moved a chair closer to the window and started hemming her dress.

"Where has Papa gone on this beautiful day"?

"He had some things to attend to, he should be back soon", Mama answered.

"I hope he remembers to bring me some more books from Strawberry school like he promised".

"You know he won't forget, Ruby, has he ever forgotten a promise to you"?

"No".

She returned to the sewing in silence.

Upon hearing the wagon she quickly laid her sewing aside and went out to meet him.

"Your books are in that satchel your mother made on the seat beside me. Since they are borrowed I didn't want to chance getting them dirty in the back".

"Oh, Papa, you always remember. From the colorful covers these look great!"

Ruby's Mountain

She carried them inside and returned to help him gather the rest of the things he had brought home.

Holding the back door open for him to go inside with his arms full, she had a steady stream of chatter about Carl and his antics. Papa laughed and agreed the boy is quite a handful.

Mama met Papa at the door and took some of his load.

"How did things go"? she asked.

"Fine, just fine. Ruby help your mother put things away, then come help me outside".

"Yes, Papa", as she wondered why his wink at Mama.

"I will help you with supper soon as I finish chores, Mama".

"That will be fine, dear, but Jewell and Sally can help peel potatoes and the apples for a pie".

"Are we celebrating something with an apple pie"? she asked.

"Just go help Papa, Ruby. He is tired and you can help him finish chores sooner."

"Yes, Mama."

Papa had finished with the wagon and watered the team. He was sitting at the picnic table in the back yard.

"Come sit down, Ruby, I have something to tell you", he called to her.

The late afternoon sun and light breeze in the trees cast long dancing shadows across the yard. Papa had laid his hat on the table and pushed his windblown hair from off his face. "How handsome he is", thought Ruby as she sat on the bench directly across the table.

"Yes, Papa?"

He took a deep breath and started.

"Ruby, your mother and I have been thinking of this for some time, and today I talked to others and they agree. Grandmother Holton would like for you and Jewell to come live with her after Christmas and go to school. Your grandmother and granddad donated the land for the school at the far end of their property, so it isn't too far for you to walk. I talked a long time with the teacher at Strawberry. She will be very glad to have you and Jewell. By the books you have been reading and the arithmetic you understand, you will be placed in the fourth grade and Jewell will be in the first. She knows her letters and is beginning to learn numbers, but she does not have the interest you have in learning. We will be coming down the mountain to see you as often as we can. You are ten now and becoming quite a grown up young lady. We are very proud of you and your help around here is great. Now it is time you get out with others and find new friends. How does that sound to you?"

"Oh, Papa". With tears streaming down her face she went around the table and hugged him so tight he could hardly breathe.

"I have wanted to go to school for a long time, but thought I was needed here more. This plan is wonderful and I will help grandmother as much as I do Mama. Oh, Papa"! She suddenly straightened up and looked toward the back door.

"What will Mama do, she needs me".

"I will be here to help. With no garden and the few cows and hogs left I will pen them up close to the house. You know there is never as much work to be done in the winter, we will make it fine".

Now she knew why the apple pie, a real celebration. When Papa told Jewell at supper, she was surprised, but didn't seem nearly as happy as Ruby.

Final plans were made and a tentative date set for her and Jewell to move down the mountain to live with Grandmother Holton.

Chapter 8

Ruby hummed softly as she, Jewell, Sally and Edna sat around the kitchen table with well used crayons and tablet paper spread before them. The silence of the softly falling snow outside was broken now and then by pellets of ice being blown against the north window by strong gusts of wind. Carl was asleep in his cradle. It had been brought in from mama and papa's bedroom and placed closer to the big wood burning cook stove.

"How are you girls doing"? Mama called from near the fireplace in the front room. She was knitting each of the girls a new pair of mittens.

Ruby's Mountain

"Our chain is getting longer and prettier", Ruby answered.

She was cutting narrow strips from the written on tablet paper Mama had saved after their lessons all fall. Edna and Sally were coloring the pages on both sides before they were cut and Jewell was pasting the strips together into connecting rings forming the chain. The flour and water paste in the bowl before her was applied to one end of the narrow strip with the end of a spent match. At times she would get too much and the paper would be too wet and not stick together. Then Jewell would have to go back and hold the ends together and blow on them to get them to stick. This made the going slow and she would get behind.

"Here, I'll help you," as Ruby picked up a strip and pasted the ends together. One chain was as long as the table and they were starting another.

"Those are pretty colors", Ruby told Edna and Sally, "they will look real pretty on the Christmas tree".

The girls looked up and smiled. Pleased with the compliment, they colored faster and faster, mixing all their colors on each page.

"Ruby, will you please stir those beans?" Mama called. "They should be done and I will be there in a little while to make some cornbread for supper. Papa should be home soon, so finish your chains and clear the table."

"OK, Mama", she replied and turned to the girls. "You heard, so lets surprise Papa and have the table cleared and set when he comes in out of this storm."

"The paste is almost gone, anyway," observed Jewell.

Ruby carefully picked up the completed chains, one at a time, and laid them on the floor against a wall in the living room near the tree. Out of the way, they could finish drying to be ready to decorate the tree in a few days.

Papa had taken Ruby and Jewell with him into the woods to pick the best cedar tree they could find before the storm. He filled an old wooden bucket with dirt and rocks to stand it in and set it in the corner away from the fireplace. He made sure it was stable and easy to reach so they could add water to keep the soil moist. The lower branches he trimmed from the tree had been turned into a lovely wreath. He had hung it securely above the mantle of the fireplace. Ruby had helped Mama make small pocket dolls and stuffed balls from colorful scraps of cloth to add to the tree's beauty.

Papa came in the back door with a loud "ho, ho, ho", waking Carl from his nap. Carl climbed out of the cradle, ran and grabbed Papa around the knees.

"Papa, Papa" he squealed.

Ruby's Mountain

"Whoa, son, let me put these things down and take my coat off." Turning, "here Ruby, you know where these go".

"Yes, Papa."

After supper and the dishes done they all went to sit around the fireplace and sang Christmas Carols.

"Why do I want to leave my beautiful family?" Ruby thought. "Grandmother has Auntie and Uncle Henry to help her. Jewell and I will just make her more work. Can I take care of Jewell and myself enough to not be too much bother?"

Her doubts and dark thoughts disappeared when Papa handed her a new book with "Read us a story, Ruby. You will be reading to Grandmother a lot when you get in school."

During the next week there was a lot of activity as well as secrecy in the home.

"Mama, can I have a piece of that pretty red cloth?"

"Mama, can I have another piece of paper?"

"Mama I need a little stick, can I go outside and get one?"

These and many more questions were asked but no one told what they needed the items for. There was always crayons and paste on the dining table for the children to use. Since everyone always ate at the same time it was easy for Ruby to clean the table before each meal. The oil cloth table cover was easy to wash and was kept clean of the colors and paste. Ruby, Jewell, Sally and Edna each had a corrugated box in their bedroom to store their creations. Carl gave his 'pictures' to Mama to keep for him.

Papa came in after doing chores Christmas Eve and asked "Is everyone ready to decorate the tree?"

"Yes" in a loud chorus.

Papa reached to the top and fastened the shiny colorful star first.

"OK", he said, "each add their own decoration after Ruby and Jewell put the chains and strings of popcorn on."

They had spent many evenings stringing popped corn with needle and thread.

Mama called them to super before they were finished. This gave them a chance to step back and admire their work so far. Few ornaments were moved after they got back to the front room to finish. Then Papa handed Ruby a folded paper and said "read this to us Ruby, Mr. John gave it to me at the store today". Ruby began to read 'Twas the Night before Christmas." The younger girls sat on a pallet on the floor and Carl came to sit on Ruby's lap. Ruby put so much feeling and expression into it that no one moved. Everyone agreed it was a beautiful poem and the 'prettiest tree they had ever seen'. They were still quiet with wonder and dreams as they went off to bed.

Christmas morning Ruby awoke to the delicious aroma of ham frying and coffee on the stove. She stretched, looked at Sally still asleep beside her. Carefully she dressed by the flicker of light from the kitchen lamp and went to help Mama get breakfast on the table. "Good morning, Mama" she said brightly as she started setting the table.

"Good morning, Ruby".

Papa came in from doing chores with a bucket of warm milk.

"Cold, but going to be a beautiful day," he told them.

Ruby took the milk, strained it through the clean cheese cloth into the churn with a lid and set it on the back porch to cool. It would go into the root cellar later to keep cool. Tomorrow after the cream comes to the top, she will bring it inside, add the dasher and churn for butter.

"Ruby the biscuits are done. Will you please go to the root cellar for some cold milk and the butter there"?

"Yes, Mama, I will wake the girls first so they can be getting dressed".

The creamy ham gravy was made and all sat down to eat. Papa said a short blessing and the chatter began. They were all anxious to see what Old St. Nick had put in their stockings they had hung on the mantle of the fireplace last night. No one was allowed to go into the living room until all could go after the table was cleared. Carl and Edna peeked around the door trying to see the tree as Ruby and Mama finished stacking the dishes on the shelf.

"Now"! Papa called from near the fireplace.

"Finally" they all exclaimed with a sigh. Four of the children hurried through the door, but Ruby hung back, savoring every moment. With mixed feelings she wanted to see what she had received, but a little sad thinking of leaving this wonderful family soon.

When they were all seated, Papa played Santa and handed each a small gift with a deep bow and a 'ho, ho, ho.'

"This is for you, Carl".

"This is for you, Edna".

"This is for you, Sally".

"This is for you, Jewell".

"And Ruby, this is for you, enjoy".

They all jumped up and tried to give him a hug at once, knocking him backward to the floor. All laughed as he picked himself up and joined in the fun.

"Oh, Papa," wept Ruby, "this book of 'Aesop's Fables' is the best gift in the whole wide world".

"Now, now, Ruby, laugh, don't cry" and patted her on the back. It has some good advice that will be helpful, as well as funny stories".

From their stockings they each pulled an orange, a few pecans, a piece of store-bought ribbon candy and a new pencil or box of crayons.

The new mittens Mama had knitted were tied to a Big Chief tablet with bright colored yarn for each and left under the tree. Then with 'oohs and oh boys' came the exchange of presents to each other they had been working on all week.

The rest of the day was enjoyed by playing games, eating popcorn balls, reading and drawing in their new tablets.

With everyone busy and not wanting dinner, Mama was in no hurry to bake the chicken and dressing until mid-afternoon. After the big early supper everyone gathered before the fireplace and sung Christmas Carols again. Ruby read 'The

Farmer and His Sons' from Aesop's Fables just before they went sleepily to bed.

What a wonderful day and the gift of family, Ruby thought as she gave Mama and Papa another hug with a thank you. She joined the girls in bed and smiling drifted off to sleep.

Chapter 9

"Ruby, I'll lay your dress here on the bed and you can hem it and sew the buttons on when you get to it. I want to finish knitting this cap for Jewell," Mama said.

"O.K. Mama, I'll do that soon as I finish this basket of ironing," Ruby answered as she lifted the iron from the cook stove. She didn't mind the mountain of clothes dampened and rolled in the basket to be ironed. She always got lost in her own thoughts and plans for the future as the ironing came automatically.

She picked up one of Edna's flowered dresses and remembered how much fun it had been to help her learn and grow. Not long after they had moved to her beautiful Pilot Rock mountain, Auntie had come to stay with them and help Mama when Edna was born. The log house was large and had an extra bedroom for her. They had all loved Auntie. She told funny stories and played with them when her chores were finished. Ruby stood on a box then to reach the table and dry dishes for her.

"Drink of water, please." Two year old Carl jerked on Ruby's skirt and brought her back to the present. She returned her iron to the stove to reheat. Picking him up, she nuzzled his neck to make him giggle, and gave him the drink. Still holding him she murmured, "I am going to miss you, bugger". The feeling of sadness yet anticipation tugged at her heart again, as it had so many times since last fall when Papa told her about starting the new chapter in her life.

"Why you cry, Ruby?" Carl asked as he searched her face. He wiped the tear running down her cheek with stubby little fingers.

"I'm just happy, Carl," as she hugged him harder again and set him down. She put his aluminum cup on the table, took the iron from the stove and started ironing again.

"How are you doing, Ruby?" Mama called from her chair in the living room.

"Fine, Mama, the basket is about half empty now, should be finished in about an hour." Ruby replied as she picked up Jewell's every day dress and started ironing. She was glad Jewell was going with her to Grandmother's. They would learn to share the chores for Grandmother like Mama had talked to them so much about. Ruby was determined to get Jewell to help more than she does at home where she often dawdles when asked to help.

Ironing finished and buttons sewn on, Ruby decided to wait until tomorrow to sew the hem in her new dress. The sun had gone down and the coal oil lamp was needed for the supper table and lessons later.

The days seemed to be flying by as Ruby, Jewell and Mama worked to get them ready for school, in addition to keeping up with regular chores.

She knew she should be inside helping Mama fix supper. Ruby had carried out the ashes from the cook stove. Balancing on the board walk Papa had laid over the mud she had dumped them into the ash hopper.

Yuck! The odor and dust that arose caused her to make a screwy face, like always. On her way back to the porch she wondered how many times she had repeated this task with the same results. Now she stood on the edge of the porch, looking around.

Ruby's Mountain

"I'm going to miss this entire farm, the unpainted out buildings, trees and even the unpleasant chores" she murmured. "Mostly though, I will miss my wonderful family and how much they depend on me." The sun was sinking lower and lower, casting long shadows in the yard and a lovely golden glow through the unmoving leafless trees toward the woods. Still she stood and gazed around as if she had never seen this place before. Lost in her memories and the silent beauty of the moment, she was surprised when Papa said, "Beautiful, isn't it?"

"Oh, yes, Papa, even more so than when we first came, if that be possible". She turned to face him and with tears in her eyes asked "Why am I so mixed up, Papa? I want to go to school and know I have to go live with Grandmother to do it. I am excited about that, but still am sad to leave my beautiful mountain home and family."

He took her by the shoulders gently as the tears started to fall.

"Ruby, girl, you are growing up and will need the education to get on in this changing world. It's not like you are leaving to go around the world. Grandmother just lives down the mountain. We will all be coming down to see you and Jewell soon. Also after the next spell of bad weather I will come get you so you can see your Pilot Rock mountain covered with the coming of spring. Like you learned in Sunday school, there is a time for everything under the sun, and now is your time to start spreading your wings. We all love you, Ruby, so don't be sad, be happy that you have this chance to learn not only from books, but how to interact with people other than family.

Handing her his big coarse handkerchief he continued. "Now dry your eyes, blow your nose, put on a smile and let's go inside to help Mama get supper.

As she lay in bed that night she thought of what Papa had said and knew he was right. She slept soundly without dreams.

Ruby sat at the sewing machine, concentrating on mending her petticoat, when Carl came and leaned against her leg.

"Please go outside, Ruby".

"Just a minute, Carl, soon as I finish this seam." She glanced at Mama who nodded her head in approval.

"The sun is bright but the wind is cold, so bundle up," she said.

Does anyone else want to go outside?" she asked the girls.

They all shouted "yes" at the same time.

Their hand-me-down coats hanging on nails on the wall were easy for them to reach. While she helped Carl, Jewell put on Ruby's last year's coat. Sally struggled into Jewell's and Edna pulled at the coat Mama had made Sally last year.

"Sally, help Edna and button her coat".

"Well, all right," she said disgustedly. Sally deliberately buttoned it uneven so Jewell stepped in and straightened it.

"Ready everybody?" Ruby asked. "When we get out the back door, go to the table and try not to step in the deep mud puddles."

At the table they discussed what to play. Each had an idea when Sally piped up with "let's play train".

"Great idea, you be the engine, then we will change at the end of the line".

Sally, Jewell, Edna, Ruby then Carl as the caboose all lined up and started chugging. Moving their arms, bent at the elbow, and shuffling their feet, they started toward the far edge of the yard. Winding first right then left they slowly gathered speed. At the end of the rocky area Ruby called "SCREEEECH" to stop them. They all shifted places with Jewell as engine and Edna as caboose. Carl didn't want to give up his position so there was a squabble to settle before returning to the 'station'.

Soon underway with the chug – chugging, the curves and whistles from the engineer the return trip was slower. Instead of stopping at the table, Jewell started running and yelling 'runaway train, runaway train'. The three girls jumped puddles and did tight curves before they neared the barnyard fence.

"SCREEEECH"! Ruby yelled and they slowly stopped. Carl had stayed by Ruby, but when they slowed he started to run, too. Ruby grabbed him just as he was about to jump into a mud puddle. He fought her and wanted down, but she held him close. The girls turned and started back. Laughing and joking they jumped the puddles in a run.

PLOP!

Edna let out a scream that could have awakened a possum in the deep woods. Ruby turned and saw Edna sitting in a mud puddle and Jewell and Sally shaking with laughter.

"Sally pushed me," Edna sobbed.

"Did not", retorted Sally, "I just barely bumped her".

"Here Jewell, take Carl and get on the porch. Sally, stay where you are".

Ruby pulled Edna out of the mud and wiped as much as she could from the back of her coat, shoes and stockings.

"Sally, did you bump her hard"?

Ruby's Mountain

She tried to keep a straight face but the twinkle in her eyes and the upward curve of the corners of her mouth gave her away when she told Ruby, "Maybe a little bit".

"Tell Edna you are sorry three times and you won't do it again," Ruby said sternly, "then you can have the pleasure of cleaning the mud from her shoes before we go inside."

"Oh, all right, but we were just playing."

"Playing is great, but think a little next time before pushing someone down. Now let's get on the back porch and clean our shoes so we won't track so much mud into the house."

Mama was standing just inside the screen door and Ruby saw her smile faintly.

The girls picked up the sticks Papa had left by the neat stack of firewood on the back porch and started scraping as much mud off their shoes as they could. They removed them and carried them inside. The next morning after they had dried behind the cook stove, they will be finished with a stiff brush.

Mama was mixing cornbread and Ruby peeling potatoes when Papa came in from the barn for dinner.

"Are you about packed and ready to go, Ruby?"

Ruby's Mountain

She hesitated and thought a minute before answering, "Yes, Papa, Jewell and I are almost packed. Why?"

"The weather is changing and I think we should plan on leaving in the morning," he replied. "Need to get there and back before the snow moves in."

Ruby quietly peeled faster and Mama beat the cornbread dough harder. Dinner was good, rather quiet as they all ate together. Papa's blessing included a special one for Ruby and Jewell and their new adventure.

Soon as the dinner table was cleared and dishes were washed and put away, Ruby and Jewell went into the bedroom and started cleaning. They pulled the sheets from the beds, picked up the younger children's toys and put them in the toy box.

"Oh, look at this, Ruby. Remember when Mama gave you this doll?"

"That was a long time ago, I didn't know it was still in the box," replied Ruby.

Jewell continued moving the toys around with an 'oh' and a giggle at rediscovering long lost items.

"Come on, Jewell, put the toys back so I can sweep. We have a lot to do before we finish our packing," Ruby urged. "You heard Papa, 'leave in the morning', and I want the whole house swept and the beds remade with clean sheets this afternoon."

"Oh, all right," as she piled the toys back in the box.

Ruby finished the sweeping in time to help Mama get supper.

With no lessons tonight, they said 'good night early.

After laying the clothes they would wear to Grandmother's tomorrow on the chair, Ruby and Jewell went to bed and slept soundly.

The big day dawned bright and cold. Papa had eaten breakfast before bringing the team and wagon close to the back yard. Ruby led the way in loading their belongings into the wagon.

"Don't forget your book satchels and the rest of the books Papa brought you, Ruby. Papa already put a new Big Chief tablet and a pencil in them," Mama told her. "The January thaw has melted the snow and ice. The rocks make the mud less slick and the road passable for now."

This day in 1906 was a turning point in her life, never to be forgotten.

With heart pounding and tears in her eyes, Ruby waved to Mama, Sally, Edna and Carl standing on the porch. Jewell, sitting on her box of clothes in the bed of the wagon behind Papa's driving seat was waving vigorously as tears flowed.

Turning in her seat beside Papa, Ruby looked up to him and exclaimed "It is such a beautiful day, Papa." He smiled as he flicked the reigns and they started down the mountain.

Chapter 10

The first night with Grandmother Holton was quiet. Ruby had settled down from her constant excited jabbering all the way down the mountain. She couldn't seem to stop urging Jewell to stop crying and to 'think of all the fun' ahead of them. This was the first time Jewell had been away from her siblings, even for a day.

Papa had taught in an Indian school in Oklahoma territory before he and Mama were married and insisted his two oldest children have an education. All the way down the mountain he just listened and paid attention to driving the team. Occasionally he put in a 'that's right', but mostly he just smiled and nodded in understanding.

When supper was over and dishes put away, Ruby followed Uncle Henry into the large room just

Ruby's Mountain

off the kitchen that was to be hers and Jewell's. She watched as he used a small shovel full of live coals from the living room fireplace to start the fire in the smaller fireplace in their room.

"You know how to bank it before you go to bed, don't you"? he asked.

"Yes" she assured him and turned to look at the lovely quilt on the large bed, the chest of drawers for their underwear, the pegs on one wall for hanging their outerwear and the wash stand with a pitcher of water and a wash pan. Hanging on the side of the wash stand were two clean wash rags and a towel. Beside the wash stand, furthest from the kitchen door was their very own slop jar with a lid. Ruby felt a surge of contentment, knowing they were welcome.

Grandmother had already picked up her knitting and was talking to Jewell when Ruby and Uncle Henry joined them by the fireplace in the living room. They laughed and talked as the howling wind blew freezing rain against the windows.

"There will be no school tomorrow", Grandmother told them as she laid aside her knitting. Miss Bertha Basham, the teacher, can't get there when ice and snow is on the road, so you can sleep as late as you like in the morning".

Jewell kissed Grandmother on the cheek and said goodnight. Ruby followed her with "thank you,

Ruby's Mountain

Grandmother, we will keep our lovely room neat and help you all we can", before saying goodnight.

Jewell was already in her flannel nightgown and in bed when Ruby came into the room. Using the small shovel, she carefully banked the fire, being sure all coals were covered with ashes so they could be easily uncovered to start a new fire in the morning. She donned her nightgown and snuggled close to Jewell. Very soon, smiling, they went sound asleep.

The storm passed in the night but for two days there was too much ice on the road to get to school. Each morning after chores were finished, breakfast over and dishes put away, the girls sat at the kitchen table and read their books and did arithmetic like Papa had taught them. Grandmother checked their numbers and answered their questions about a story if they did not understand or didn't know a word.

When Jewell started squirming and whining Ruby said, "Oh, all right, you have done enough for now".

Grandmother came into the kitchen when Ruby was adding the books to their satchels. She started singing and Ruby joined in. Soon all three were singing and dancing as they peeled potatoes and started cooking dinner.

After supper Ruby read stories to Grandmother and Uncle Henry from her Aesop's

Ruby's Mountain

Fables. Uncle Henry then told some stories of his own, complete with waving arms and facial expressions. Everyone laughed and enjoyed the evening.

The third day Grandmother hitched the team to the buggy bundled the girls in a blanket and drove them through the mud to school.

"I will come get you after school", she said.

"Thank you, Grandmother".

She was in the line of wagons and buggies waiting to pick up children at the front door of the one room school.

"What a day!" Ruby exclaimed as they climbed into the buggy to go home.

The teacher had taken time for each individual student, grades one through six, to help with their assignments. Since the school yard was so muddy they were not allowed out except to walk to the outdoor toilet on the straw paths some of the parents had made. The boys had kept the fire going in the big wood burning stove in the middle of the room. Parents had brought wood and stacked it in the cloak room before the storm hit.

For exercise at recess, they marched around the room as they sang songs. They played musical chairs to the teacher's singing. Jewell whined when she was first to lose her chair.

Ruby's Mountain

Ruby was glad they had cleaned their room before school and helped Grandmother fix supper. They discussed the school day some more as they ate. Ruby read another story to all and saying she was tired, said goodnight and went to bed where Jewell was already fast asleep.

Chapter 11

"Jewell, look! Papa's horse is tied to the hitching post at Grandmother's" Ruby exclaimed. The sun was shining and they had been poking along as they walked from school. They were looking for tiny Johnny-jump-ups beside the dirt road. Seeing Papa's horse woke them up and with coat tails flapping and book satchels bouncing with every step, they raced toward the house. The back door was open and the screen door slammed behind them as they ran to Papa. He was sitting at the table with a cup of coffee. He stood and held both of the girls tightly.

"When did you get here?"

"How's Mama?"

"Does Sally miss me?"

"I'll bet baby Carl has grown a lot."

The questions came too fast for him to answer.

"Whoa", he said. "Sit down and I will tell you about all of them."

They sat down as he told them that they were all OK and asked about Jewell and Ruby both every day.

"They sent you these pictures and letters they made for you and Mama knitted you both new caps", he said as he handed the things to each of them.

Ruby told him how much she liked school and how she was helping the teacher by helping the younger children with their reading. Jewell opened her book satchel and showed him the good grades marked on her arithmetic papers.

Soon he stood and announced that he had to go to get up the mountain before dark. Before he mounted his horse he told them to be ready next Saturday morning and he will come get them to spend the night and see how the mountain is 'beginning to wake up' from the bad winter.

"We'll be ready", they said at the same time.

When supper was over, neither of them hesitated in getting started on their homework. Ruby finished studying her spelling and numbers.

Ruby's Mountain

"Grandmother, the teacher asked the fourth, fifth and sixth grade students about where our families were from. Can you tell me about you, Grandpa and Papa"?

"Well, Ruby", laying her knitting aside she said, "I can tell you a story about your Grandpa that I know is true".

She told them about how they were living near Sparta, Tennessee when the Civil War was going on. The neighbors, though far apart, would warn each other when there were Union soldiers in the area. Your Grandpa's family would hide him in a creek where the roots of a big tree came out over the water. He stayed in the water close to the bank under those roots until the soldiers left the area. Before they left, though, they went into the house and took the feather beds outside. Tying the corners to the saddle horn with a rope they then cut holes in the other end of the feather bed and ran up and down the road on their horses until the feathers were all out of the ticking. They laughed as the feathers scattered to the wind. They went to the smokehouse to get the meat hanging to be smoked. They were surprised to see the family throwing the meat into the garden. When the Officers demanded why, the family told them they thought the meat had been poisoned. The soldiers then searched until they found the dried fruit and beans. Cutting holes in the sacks, they emptied them into the big water well.

Ruby's Mountain

Ruby and Jewell sat in complete silence as Grandmother continued with her story.

Your Grandpa and I were married shortly after the war ended. We stayed on the farm and your Papa was born there.

When he was fourteen, we packed up everything we had and left Tennessee. My sister, Auntie Mary Bradley, came with us and was a great help to everyone. We traveled in a covered wagon pulled by a team of strong mules. We crossed the Mississippi river on a split log barge into Missouri. After resting a few days we came south into Arkansas. We bought this land in the valley north of Clarksville and built this big log house. The soil was rich so we had a big garden for plenty of vegetables. We built the big barn and pen for the livestock. The lush pasture has a creek running through, so there was plenty of water for the animals. Your Strawberry school was later built on the far end of our land.

"Your Grandpa didn't like farming." Grandmother finished," so when he got me and the children, six boys and a girl, settled, he went to California to make his fortune in the gold mines."

Remembering fondly, she paused and smiled.

"He got sick and came back to us. He didn't live much longer and I have never moved."

"Thank you, Grandmother", said Ruby.

Ruby's Mountain

"Did the family have anything left to eat after throwing their meat out"? asked Jewell.

"Yes, after they were sure the soldiers were gone from the area, they picked up the meat, washed the dirt off and hung it back in the smokehouse. They built a fire in the pit in the middle of the floor then cut young hickory trees and smoked the meat as usual. Time for bed, girls, sleep well".

Ruby and Jewell kissed Grandmother on the cheek and with a quiet 'goodnight' went to bed.

Chapter 12

"Whoa",

Papa said as he pulled on the reins at the back yard. Screaming, Jewell jumped out the back of the wagon before it had come to a complete stop and ran to Sally and Edna, who were screaming and running toward her. Carl could not keep up and was almost knocked down when the girls collided.

Ruby stood in front of the spring seat, breathing deeply, to keep her emotions from showing. She looked around, remembering and enjoying that old feeling of love and contentment she always had about this Pilot Rock mountain home. Lost in the warm sunshine and beauty of the day, she didn't see Papa standing beside the wagon with outstretched hand to help her down until he spoke her name.

"Oh, Papa, this is still such a wonderful, magical place," she whispered as he set her on the ground.

"Yes," he agreed, the past five years living here has been good".

Ruby saw Mama standing on the porch and hurried to her, scooping Carl up in her arms on the way. Mama put her arms around Ruby and Carl before she spoke.

"So good to see you, Ruby. We have missed you, haven't we Carl?"

He giggled and clung around Ruby's neck even tighter as if to agree.

"Come help me get dinner on the table. I want to hear all about school and your Grandmother and Uncle Henry," she said.

The big wood burning cook stove keeping the food warm also made the kitchen very comfortable and warmed Ruby after the ride from Grandmothers. She kept up a constant chatter as she put the meal on the table.

"Oh, you baked an apple pie! You know how much I love it, don't you, Mama"?

Turning, she noticed Mama had sat down and was letting Ruby do all the work.

"What's wrong, Mama?" she asked. "You aren't feeling well".

"I'm just a little tired, nothing to worry about. I want this to be a special time for you and Jewell."

The back door burst open and in ran the three girls. Jewell ran to hug Mama while Sally and Edna ran to Ruby for a 'hello' hug. They were all talking at once when Papa came in after unhitching and watering the team.

"I'm starved!" he stated with enthusiasm.

Following Papa's prayer of thanks and blessings, the meal was enjoyed by all, ending with the apple pie. Ruby noticed Mama, who was always a light eater, ate even less and had to excuse herself to go outside to the toilet. Ruby looked questioningly at Papa, but he didn't seem concerned.

After the girls finished the dishes they again put on coats and went outside for Mama and Papa to show them how the flowers and early garden vegetables were coming through the cold ground.

After dinner Sunday, following a very pleasant two days, Papa took Ruby and Jewell down the mountain again to Grandmother's. Jewell did not cry all the way this time, but kept pointing out to Papa and Ruby how all the trees were budding and seemed to change the color of the whole forest.

Ruby's Mountain

"I will see you again soon," Papa promised as he clicked to the team to start back up the mountain. Grandmother had joined Ruby and Jewell to wave as he pulled onto the road. Ruby noticed and wondered as he went in the opposite direction from the way they came in, but said nothing.

"Here, Grandmother, is a jar of honey Mama sent you".

"Thank you, Ruby. Now come inside where it is out of the wind and warmer. I want to hear about your weekend and how is your Mama"?

As they entered the kitchen, they were really surprised to see Auntie standing there to meet them.

"Auntie"! Ruby and Jewell exclaimed at once and ran quickly to give her a hug. "It is so good to see you"!

Grandmother and Auntie with a cup of coffee and Ruby and Jewell with a glass of milk sat at the kitchen table. Ruby told them about Mama not feeling well, but insisting they eat and enjoy the weekend. They laughed and visited until time to get supper. Uncle Henry came through and grabbed a cookie on his way to the barn for evening chores.

After supper Ruby read from her school book to them, then stories from her Aesop's Fables. Auntie was very pleased to see how much better she could read than when she had worked with Ruby on the mountain. Jewell also read a little, then showed her how she could do numbers now.

The signs of spring were more evident every day. The lettuce and radishes Grandmother had planted in a small patch in the protected corner of the fenced garden on Valentine's Day were almost ready to eat. Uncle Henry plowed the rest of the garden so Ruby and Jewell could help Grandmother plant after school. As they went down the rows dropping potato eyes, March 15, Ruby called words to Jewell to spell.

"You are doing real good", Ruby told her. "Keep it up and you could win the spelling bee coming up next week."

Papa showed up one Saturday in the wagon. They were glad to see him, but why the wagon? They sat around the kitchen table while Papa explained.

"I came to get Auntie to help your Mama. I have a big farm with a big house over by Hagarville. You girls will be going to Salem school then which is a little closer for you to walk. It is a bigger school with classes going through the ninth grade. Ruby, you will be able to help the teacher more, too. We are moving a few things every day, but your Mama needs help while packing and taking care of the kids. Ruby, you and Jewell will stay here and help Grandmother and keep up the good work in school."

Ruby's Mountain

"But, Papa."

He held up his hand to stop her. "I will come get you when school lets out for planting in about a month. You will be able to help Mama and Auntie put things away. There is a lot of plowing and planting to do there, too, Ruby. Do you think you can help me in the fields and garden?"

"Of course, Papa," she answered," but couldn't I go with you now to help move?"

Auntie came in with her box of clothes. Papa stood and promising to see them before long, said good bye.

The next weekend Grandmother took Ruby and Jewell to watch Mr. Pitts, a neighbor, bore holes in his sugar maple trees. She followed him from one tree to the next as he hammered drain pipes into the holes so the sap dripped into buckets hung on the end of the pipes.

"Won't this kill the trees?" Ruby asked.

"No," he answered and showed them the scars on the trees from last year's harvest. "They seal over fast when the pipes are taken out".

He already had several buckets collected and some ladies were in the process of cooking it. They had two iron kettles over green oak fires, one for brown sugar and one for maple syrup. The four ladies, two for each kettle, stirred constantly with long handle wooden paddles.

"Why do you have to keep stirring?" Ruby asked as she watched, fascinated.

"To keep it from scorching and to help the liquid evaporate faster," one lady told her. "Scorched maple syrup doesn't taste good on a hot biscuit with lots of butter. Do you like biscuits and syrup for breakfast?"

Ruby laughed and said, "Oh, yes, and at other times, too."

Chapter 13

Ruby drowsily turned over in bed as she heard a pecking on the window. She vaguely wondered what it was, and then sat straight up in bed, wide awake.

"Jewell," she shook her sister. "It is snowing and sleeting and we are late for school and our room is a mess and my hair's not combed!"

The words tumbled out in a stream.

Grandmother who was in the kitchen, heard her and came to the door of their room.

"It's OK Ruby, no school today. The snow has been coming down like this most all night. The ice pellets that are mixed with it will not let it melt any time soon."

Ruby fell back on her pillow with a groan and closed her eyes. This close to the end of the school year and going back home to the family, this weather was not welcome. What a change from last week when it was so warm and bright when we went to watch Mr. Pitts drill the holes in his sugar maples. She hoped Papa got everything moved, but it would be a while before he could come get her and Jewell. She was ready to cry in self-pity when Jewell turned over and asked her what was wrong.

"I was just being ungrateful for this beautiful snow", she told Jewell. "This ice and snow will make us late getting out of school and Papa won't be back as soon as he promised."

"Get dressed and I will fix your breakfast," Grandmother told them. "Then we will do some lessons. I will help you."

In the afternoon the snow started tapering off, but it was too cold to get outside. Grandmother helped Ruby mend a dress that had a rip while Jewell sat in front of the fireplace on the floor lost in her own dreams.

Uncle Henry went to the barn to look after the animals. He broke the ice on the watering trough, milked the cows and gathered the eggs and hurried back to the warmth of the kitchen. There was plenty of wood stacked on the back porch for the cook stove and fireplaces. He warmed a few minutes and drank a cup of hot coffee before going out again to draw water from the well. After several trips to the well through the deep snow, he was ready for supper.

"You are a walking snowman", Ruby teased.

She took his wet coat, cap and gloves to hang on the clothes line in back of the cook stove.

He laughed.

A lump came in her throat, he sounded so much like Papa.

After supper Ruby and Jewell sang songs they had learned in school while doing the dishes. When the kitchen was clean, they joined Grandmother and Uncle Henry by the fireplace in the front room.

Grandmother, sitting in her chair near the coal oil lamp, took her bible from the small table and read them the story of Easter. She told them this weather was the Easter storm that happened every year at this time. She followed by telling them the legend of the dogwood tree. It is said, the dogwood tree once was standing tall and straight in the forest. The wood was used for the cross but ever since then it is shorter, gnarled and with many branches. The white blossoms with four petals have blood on the tips.

Ruby's Mountain

The girls listened, fascinated. They had heard the story many times in Sunday school, but it had never been as personal as Grandmother explained it.

Days later Grandmother took them to school in the buggy and picked them up afterwards to prevent their wading the mud. Papa was waiting for them when they got home.

"I've been to the mountain to finally finish bringing the rest of our things down," he told them. "I was too late. Someone had stayed in the house, which was fine, but they burned it down, which wasn't fine. Mama's spinning wheel, loom and all her wool was in the house, as well as some things she had made for you girls."

His voice broke and he looked away before saying, "The storm kept me from getting there sooner."

Ruby and Jewell listened and blinked back tears. It was to Ruby, the end of a beautiful time on her beloved Pilot Rock mountain. She would welcome the new home, though, and not dwell on what had happened. She told Papa she was glad no one was hurt.

This session of school ended about a month later. Ruby and Jewell had their clothes, books and personal items packed in the cardboard boxes they had brought them in, ready to go, when Papa picked them up.

Ruby's Mountain

The beautiful spring day with birds singing, flowers blooming, grass and garden vegetables showing growth was a joy for Ruby to see. It all seemed to come together – another spring and a new home.

"Such a beautiful day, Papa," Ruby told him after saying their goodbyes and thank you to Grandmother and Uncle Henry.

Sally, Edna and Carl were waiting for them when Papa pulled up to the big log house. Mama was on the porch to welcome them with open arms.

Ruby stood and looked around. Seeing Mama, her heart sank. As Papa gave her his hand to climb down from the wagon, she had mixed feelings. At eleven she knew she was no longer a child and would have to take on more responsibilities for her family.

Chapter 14

Gresham was born shortly after Ruby and Jewell moved home from Grandmothers. She was so glad Auntie was staying to help Mama.

The day they arrived had been spent visiting and playing with the younger ones. Carl followed at Ruby's heels from room to room, chatting in his own three year old language. He told her about how he loves Gresham and talks to him to make him laugh. Sally and Edna latched on to Jewell, following her and begging her to come outside "to see our new playhouse".

"Ruby, are you ready to hoe in the garden today? The spinach and mustard greens are ready

Ruby's Mountain

to pull for Mama and Auntie to can, then we will spade up that area and plant turnips", he said.

"Yes, Papa", as she came into the kitchen carrying the new bonnet Mama had made her. "Will you get me started?"

"I will do the spading when I come in for dinner, so you just pull the greens and get them to the house this morning. Jewell will help you."

The grass in the middles between the rows of vegetables had really grown. By middle of the afternoon she was using the hoe to chop it out as well as in the rows. Jewell was helping wash the greens, so Sally would take Ruby fresh drinks of water. Edna was made to feel like she was helping by playing with Carl while Gresham slept. Ruby was so pleased to see everyone pitching in, even though she got awfully tired and fell in bed and was asleep soon after supper.

"Papa, it is raining and there is no place to go to get out of it!" Ruby yelled.

Papa was faster at chopping the cotton, so was ahead of her in the next row.

"Just keep working, Ruby, girl. Look at the clouds; see how fast they are moving and how small they are? This is only a summer shower and won't last but a few minutes, not even long enough to get the ground soaked. It's late so we will go inside when we get to the end of these rows and start again in the morning. The geese have done a good job of clearing the crab grass so we can see cotton and the thinning goes faster", he told her.

The 23 big blue geese Papa kept in a lot close to the house at night were turned into the cotton patch each morning. They ate the crab grass as they went to and from the water at the far end of the field that Papa set out for them every afternoon late.

The cotton plants had to be thinned to 8 to 10 inches apart when they were 6 to 12 inches tall. At maturity they were 3 to 4 feet tall, bushy and lots of leaves, so needed space to expand. This took Papa and Ruby several days to chop the 16 acres he had planted.

"School starts tomorrow," Papa announced when he came in from the store in Hagarville. The crops were laid by and work had eased. The daily chores continued and Ruby had started helping with milking the 6 cows they kept for milk and butter.

"Oh, I will be so glad to get back to the books. Will Sally go with Jewell and me to Salem school"? she asked Papa.

"Yes, I have talked to the first grade teacher and she said to let her come. You and Jewell will pick up where you left off at Strawberry. This session will only be about two months long so the children can all help with the harvest. I will take

Ruby's Mountain

you in the morning to be sure you know the way", Papa told her.

Mama had made all three of the girls a new book satchel to take. They were assigned seats in the section reserved for each grade. The teacher took turns with each class.

Ruby's group would each stand and read a paragraph aloud from their history book. One day as they read the lesson everyone laughed. Mattie was reading when Lois reached over and pulled her skirt down. Mattie turned and in a loud voice said, "I'm going to slam your head against a tree for that." Lois ran out of the school house and all the way to her home without stopping. Ruby turned red in the face in embarrassment for her friend.

Mama never regained her health completely after Gresham was born. Ruby took on more of the work at home, helping Papa in the field as well as helping the teacher at school. Auntie would come for short stays, mostly at canning times. Ruby always told her how glad she was to see her and how much she appreciated her help. Ruby realized Auntie was growing older and couldn't do as much as she once could. Whereas, Ruby was growing in size and was taking on more responsibility as time went by. Still Papa insisted Ruby go to each session of school.

Ruby and Pearl had become friends at school and shared work experiences they had at home. One day Pearl told Ruby how she and her brother played jokes on each other. Herbert had pulled a good one on Pearl. To get him back, when she was doing the washing she had starched his long johns (winter underwear) real stiff. When they dried hanging on the clothes line, she stood them up in his closet. Ruby could imagine the expression on his face when he saw them. Both the girls had a good laugh.

Ruby was twelve years old that cold blustery day in February, 1908, when her mother was laid to rest in the Hagarville cemetery. Mama's wedding ring shone through the dainty white crocheted gloves and her face was blue. As a cloud came over the sun Ruby shivered.

"She is cold, Papa, see how blue her hands are?" Ruby whispered.

Silently he took Ruby's hand and squeezed it gently. "You are going to have to help me, Ruby. You know how to take care of the other children".

The five siblings had been left with a neighbor while Ruby and Papa had gone to the cemetery to lay her mother to rest.

"Yes, Papa," she replied as he held her hand tightly and returned to the wagon, just the two of them.

As he tucked the homespun blanket around her, she could see the pain in his face and the red eyes. She had so many questions but knew instinctively he wasn't able to answer them now. In her mind she kept asking herself if she did not do enough to help Mama. What happened? The doctor was there and said he was doing all he could. I kept the kids in my bedroom like Papa said.

Ruby saw big tears roll down Papa's cheek as they bounced along in the spring-board. Looking away, she retreated into memories of fun time with her mother.

"Ruby," her mother called.

"Yes, Mama".

We need to make you another dress for school. I've been saving these pretty flour sacks just for you."

"Thank you, Mama".

They stretched a sheet tightly over the top of the bedspread on which to lay the sacks. Mama showed her how to lay the pattern so she didn't waste any material. Laying the case knives on the pattern pieces to hold them in place, Ruby picked up the scissors.

The wagon hit a big bump in the rocky road, jarring Ruby back to the present. She looked around. Her heart ached for Papa; she had never seen him cry before. Pulling the blanket up to her neck she quietly continued her memories.

Ruby's Mountain

Whacking away at the fabric, not very carefully, Ruby started cutting the dress.

"Slow down, Ruby, these pieces you are cutting out have to fit together"

"Yes, Mama."

The bright summer day was beautiful and Ruby wanted to be outside playing with Jewell, Edna, Sally and Carl.

The precious times with her mother flooded in and she smiled, faintly. As she glanced again at Papa in his grief, she realized most of her earlier memories were of being with him. Seems he had always depended on her help and companionship.

Like when they lived on Pilot Rock Mountain, the cattle roamed free in the woods and had to be checked occasionally. On one of their outings to leave a block of salt for the cows, they found something on a tree stump that looked like jelly.

"What is that?" Ruby had asked.

"A star from heaven" was all he would say.

She never questioned or found out exactly what it was.

"Whoa"

The wagon stopped and Ruby climbed down to go inside and hold the children close. The house seemed so empty. She went into her room, lay across her bed and sobbed quietly.

Epilogue

Grandmother Holton came to live with Papa and the children not long after Mama passed away. Ruby continued her education at Salem school through the ninth grade and helped Papa on the farm.

Salem school remained the gathering place of the community. Ruby was treasurer of her Sunday school class there. She met Sherman Bean there at one of the Saturday night 'singings'. He winked at her through the reflection of the large mirror hanging on the wall behind the piano. He walked her home from every meeting that weather permitted and wrote her notes when she couldn't go.

They were married at her home February 1, 1914, when both were 18.

She had six children, worked hard and had a long full life, outliving all her siblings. She passed away in January, 1989, with her children by her side.

Ruby's Mountain

ABOUT THE AUTHOR

Houstine Cooper has been interested in writing since childhood. Writing short stories, poetry, entering and winning the "25 words or less" contests was her passion for many years. Married to a professional Air Force man in 1946, she kept packing boxes in the back room, ready to move with the least notice.

The poem 'Phone Conversation' in the book of poetry "Many an I Love You" was written following the death of her son-in-law. It won a third place in a National Library of Poetry contest.

Now retired, she is an accomplished needle tatter and author. She also keeps busy with family, friends and her church.

Books by Houstine Cooper:

Tatting ABC's and 123's
Many an I Love You
Lifespan of a Leaf
Ruby's Mountain